THE ULTIMATE

VEGETARIAN

AIR FRYER

COOKBOOK

2022

Delicious and Easy Meatless, Weight Loss Recipes to Fry, Bake & Roast

For Beginners and Advanced Users on a Budget with Step by Step Instructions

CHRIS JAPALINO

TABLE OF CONTENT

CHAPTER TWO: LUNCH & DINNER...27

CHAPTER THREE: SIDES & SNACKS...48

CHAPTER FOUR: DESSERTS...59

CHAPTER FIVE: WEIGHT LOSS...70

CHAPTER SIX: JUICE & SMOOTHIES...82

INTRODUCTION

Vegetarianism is the practice of avoiding meat and fish consumption for moral, religious, or health reasons. In comparison to meat eaters, vegetarians had lower blood pressure, lower levels of low-density lipoprotein cholesterol, and decreased incidences of hypertension and type 2 diabetes. They also had a lower BMI, a decreased chance of chronic disease, and a lower overall cancer rate.

Vegetarians come in a variety of forms:

1. Lacto-Ovo is a combination of lactose and ovo Vegetarians are those who do not eat meat, fish, or poultry but do consume dairy and eggs. Grains, fruits, and vegetables, legumes (dry beans, peas, and lentils), seeds, nuts, dairy products, and eggs were the mainstays.

2. Lacto Vegetarian: This is a type of vegetarianism in which meat, poultry, seafood, and eggs are not consumed. Meat, fish, poultry, and eggs, as well as foods containing them, are not allowed in the diet. Milk, cheese, yogurt, and butter are among the dairy products they consume.

3. Ovo Vegetarian: This is a style of vegetarianism that accepts egg consumption but not dairy consumption. Meat, poultry, seafood, and dairy items are not allowed in the diet, however eggs are allowed.

4. Pescatarian: A pescatarian diet excludes meat, poultry, dairy, and eggs while allowing fish.

5. Vegan: Those who avoid eating any animal-derived goods such as gelatin, honey, eggs, or dairy. Meat, poultry, fish, eggs, and dairy products, as well as foods contained in these products, are not included in the diet.

This incredible cookbook contains 6 categories of delectable air fryer recipes. The categories are as follows:

BREAKFAST

LUNCH & DINNER

SIDES AND SNACKS

DESSERTS

WEIGHT LOSS

JUICE & SMOOTHIES.

SOME COMMON VEGETARIAN KITCHEN CONDIMENTS

Here are some of the common vegetarian ingredients that should be available in the kitchen of a vegetarian.

*Ketchup

*Mustard

*Vegan Mayonnaise

*Soy Sauce

*Tahini

*Hot Sauce

*BBQ Sauce

*Sour Cream

*Vegan Worcestershire Sauce

*Horseradish

*Baking powder

*Baking soda

*Chili sauce

*Apple sauce

*Seitan

*Dried fruits

*Nut butter

*Oils

*Sweetener

*Sea salt

*Citrus fruits

*Dried and canned beans

*Coconut milk

*Potatoes

*Onions

*Canned Artichokes

*Tomatoes

*Nutritional yeast

*Oats

*Pumpkins

*Pepper

*Vanilla extract

*Dried herbs and spices

*Flours

*Fresh veggies

*Tofu and temph

*Vegan cheese

*Miso

*Non-diary milk

AIR FRYER

An air fryer is a new type of kitchen gadget that is widely used across the world. It is a small oven that can grill, roast, fry, and bake while using less fat. The surprise aspect is that it transports heat via air, making it healthier. It is really quick, simple, and convenient to use. Food prepared in an air fryer is always attractive and delicious, and you will find it difficult to refuse.

BENEFITS OF COOKING WITH AIR FRYER

* Healthier and Low-fat meals:

The air fryer can be used without any oil or with only a small amount of fat. It is both healthy and impressive as a result of these factors.

*Quicker meals: Because the air fryer is smaller than an oven, it saves time and allows you to eat your food quickly.

*Easy to operate: Air fryers are simple to use. Simply set the temperature and cooking time, then add the meal and shake a few times during the cooking process.

*Easy to clean: An air fryer is incredibly easy to clean; most of us dislike cleaning when cooking, but trust me on this. You only have to clean a pan and a basket.

*Adaptability: An air fryer can be used for a variety of purposes. Cooking methods include grilling, baking, roasting, and frying.

AIR FRYER MAINTENANCE

1. Unplug the air fryer before cleaning it, and let it cool completely before cleaning it.

2. Remove the plate, basket, and any other removable items and wash them in the dishwasher or by hand with warm water, a gentle sponge, and soap.

3. Use a moist sponge or towel to clean the inside, controls, and outside of the air fryer machine. It is important to note that the use of soap is not suggested.

4. The heating element is cleaned according to the user manual's instructions. Clean with a brush or a nonabrasive cloth every now and again.

5. Allow all pieces to dry thoroughly before reassembling.

HEALTHY TIPS FOR AIR FRYER

Any appliance can provide a risk, which can be avoided by following simple safety guidelines.

It has the potential to be extremely effective in lowering the likelihood of future unplanned events. These safety precautions, as simple as they may seem, can be quite valuable and can be utilized for practically all of the appliances you use on a regular basis at home.

1. Carefully read the air fryer's instruction manual: The manual offers important information about how to use the appliance properly. The manual contains step-by-step instructions as well as visual representations that make operating the air fryer simple.

2. Do not use the air fryer in a non-ventilated environment; when operating the air fryer, open the windows as wide as possible if necessary, do not set it against a wall, and switch on the vent hood.

3. Nothing should be placed on top of the air fryer.

4. Keep the power cable away from water and hot surfaces.

5. To avoid burning yourself, always wear a silicone glove.

6. Fill the air fryer basket equally with food (do not overcrowd it).

7. Preheat the air fryer before using it: When using an air fryer, don't expect a miracle by simply tossing the food in. To get a nice result, you should warm it for 10 minutes before putting the meal inside.

8. Keep youngsters and pets away.

9. Use a fair amount of oil: pouring more oil than is required can be dangerous; it can result in a fire hazard, which is bad for your kitchen. The air fryer, on the other hand, achieves a crispiness level without using much oil.

10. Do not attempt to fix it on your own.

MEASUREMENTS AND CONVERSIONS

Measurement conversion scale

Dash = 1/16 teaspoon

Pinch = 1/8 teaspoon

1 tablespoon = 3 teaspoons

1 cup = 16 tablespoons

1 cup =8 ounces

1 pound = 16 ounces

1 pint = 2 cups

1 quart = 2 pint or 4 cups

1 gallon = 16 cups

1 ml =1/5 teaspoon

1 teaspoon = 5 ml

1 ounce = 30 ml

1 cup = 240 ml

1 ounce = 28 grams

1 pound = 454 grams

1 liter = 34 ounces

100 grams = 3.5 ounces

1 kilogram = 22 pounds or 35 ounces

4 tablespoon = 1/4 cups

16 tablespoons = 1 cup

2 cups = 16 ounces

1 quart = 32 ounces = 2 pint

Units Abbreviations and Meanings

pkg. =package

oz. = ounce

med. = medium

tsp. = teaspoon

Tbsp. tablespoon

Pinch =1/8 tablespoon. A little more than a dash. Take a little between your thumb and forefinger.

Dash = a small amount. A little less than a pinch

lb. = pound

CHAPTER ONE

BREAKFAST

Sweet Polenta Fries

Prep time: 4 mins Cook time: 30 mins Total time: 34 mins Servings: 4

INGREDIENTS

1 package prepared polenta

Salt and ground black pepper to taste

Nonstick olive oil cooking spray

DIRECTIONS

STEP 1

Preheat the air fryer to 360°F (175 degrees C).

STEP 2

Cut polenta into long, thin slices that resemble french fries.

STEP 3

In the bottom of the air fryer basket, spray some olive oil. Half of the polenta should be placed in the basket, and the tops should be lightly sprayed with cooking spray. Salt & pepper to taste.

STEP 4

Cook for a total of ten minutes. Cook for 5 minutes, turning the fries with a spatula until crispy.

STEP 5

Place the fries on a paper towel-lined dish. Carry on with the second half of the fries.

Easy Hard Boiled Eggs

Prep Time: 2 mins Cook Time: 16 mins Total Time: 18 mins Servings: 2

INGREDIENTS

6 medium eggs

DIRECTIONS

STEP 1

Set the wire rack inside the basket of air fryer and put the eggs on top. Set the air fryer temperature to 250 and the timer to 16 minutes.

STEP 2

When it's time, Remove and put them in a bowl filled with ice water to stop the cooking.

STEP 3

Peel the eggs and enjoy!

Fresh Oatmeal

Prep Time: 7 mins Cook Time: 20 mins Total Time: 27 mins Servings: 4

INGREDIENTS

1 cup of milk

1 egg

1/3 teaspoon of salt

1/6 cup of brown sugar

2 cup of strawberries, diced

1 cup of rolled oats

1/2 teaspoon of baking powder

1/2 teaspoon of ground cinnamon

1/8 cup of slivered almonds

DIRECTIONS

STEP 1

Firstly, mix the egg and milk in a bowl.

STEP 2

Mix the oatmeal, brown sugar, salt, baking powder, cinnamon in another bowl and mix thoroughly.

STEP 3

Spray air fryer safe pan with olive oil, place 1/3 cup of strawberries at the bottom. Firstly, pour the oatmeal mixtures in, and then pour the egg and milk mixture over it. Let sit for about 10 minutes. Add some more strawberries on top.

STEP 4

Sprinkle with almonds and nutmeg. Place the pan in the air fryer and set the temperature for 330 degrees F, for 10 minutes.

STEP 5

When it's time, remove from the air fryer, and let sit for 5 minutes before serving.

Vegetarian Baby Potatoes

Prep Time: 4 mins Cook Time: 20 mins Total Time: 24 mins Servings: 4

INGREDIENTS

1 1.5 pound bag baby red potatoes

1 tablespoon olive oil

3 tablespoons melted butter

1 teaspoon sea salt

1/2 teaspoon fresh cracked pepper

1 tablespoon fresh chopped parsley

DIRECTIONS

STEP 1

Place the potatoes in a clean big basin after rinsing and patting them dry, then drizzle with olive oil and season with salt.

STEP 2

Transfer the potatoes into the air fryer. Set air fryer temperature to 380 degrees and cook for 20 minutes. Remove the basket midway through the cooking process and shake it.

STEP 3

Place potatoes in serving dish. Stir in the butter, salt, pepper, and parsley, and toss to combine. Serve right away.

Coconut French Toast

Prep time: 3 mins Cook Time: 4 mins Total Time: 7 mins Serving: 1

INGREDIENTS

2 Slices of Gluten-Free Bread

1/2 Cup Lite Culinary Coconut Milk

1/2 Cup Unsweetened Shredded Coconut

1 tablespoon Baking Powder

DIRECTIONS

STEP 1

In a medium bowl, mix together the baking powder and coconut milk.

STEP 2

Spread the shredded coconut out on a clean plate.

STEP 3

Soak each slice of bread in the coconut milk mixture for few seconds before putting it into the shredded coconut plate. Fully coating the slice bread.

STEP 4

Place coated bread in the air fryer, allowing space in between. Set the temperature to 350 degrees F and 4 minutes.

STEP 5

Once its time, take them out and top with favorite French toast toppings!

Morning Granola Bars

Prep Time: 4 mins Cook Time: 15 mins Total Time: 19 mins Servings: 6

INGREDIENTS

250 g Gluten Free Oats

1 teaspoon Vanilla Essence

1 teaspoon Cinnamon

Handful Raisins

3 tablespoon Honey

1 Medium Peeled & Cooked Apple

1 teaspoon Olive Oil

60 g Melted Butter

30 g Brown Sugar

DIRECTIONS

STEP 1

Add the gluten free oats into a blender and blend until smooth, add the rest of the dry ingredients into blender.

STEP 2

Add the wet ingredients in the air fryer baking pan and stir well with a wooden spoon.

STEP 3

Pour the dry ingredients in the blender into the baking pan and mix well with a spoon. Put the raisins and press down the mixture into the baking pan, smooth the top to level.

STEP 4

Set the air fryer temperature to 160c/320f. Cook for 10 minutes, check and cook further 5 minutes at 180c/360f.

STEP 5

Remove and Put in the freezer for 5 minutes.

STEP 6

Chop into granola bars and serve.

Irresistible Tofu Scramble

Prep Time: 4 mins Cook Time: 30 mins Total Time: 34 mins Servings: 3

INGREDIENTS

1 block tofu, chopped into 1 inch chunk

Cups broccoli florets

2 tablespoons soy sauce

1/2 teaspoon garlic powder

1/2 cup chopped onion

1 tablespoon olive oil

1 teaspoon turmeric

2 1/2 cups chopped red potato, cut into 1 inch chunk

4 1/3 teaspoon onion powder

DIRECTIONS

STEP 1

In a medium mixing bowl, combine the tofu, olive oil, soy sauce, garlic powder, turmeric, onion powder, and onion. Put aside to marinate

STEP 2

Toss the potatoes in the olive oil in the second small bowl and air fry for 15 minutes at 380°F, shaking after 7 minutes.

STEP 3

When it's time, give it another good shake, then add the tofu, reserving the marinade. Cook the tofu and potatoes for another 15 minutes at 380°F.

STEP 4

Toss the broccoli in the leftover marinade in the meantime. Around 5 minutes before the end of the cooking time, add the broccoli to the air fryer and cook it all together.

STEP 5

When everything is ready, serve and enjoy.

Quick Corn Muffins

Prep Time: 7 mins Cook Time: 13 mins Total Time: 20 mins Servings: 4

INGREDIENTS

1 cup flour

1 teaspoon baking soda

2 large eggs

1/4 cup sugar

1 cup yellow cornmeal

1 teaspoon salt

1 tablespoon baking powder

1 1/4 cups buttermilk

1/3 cup vegetable oil

Olive oil

DIRECTIONS

STEP 1

Mix together the flour, baking powder, yellow cornmeal, salt, baking soda, and sugar in a large mixing bowl. Add and mix in the eggs, buttermilk and vegetable oil.

STEP 2

Spray the air fryer muffin cup with olive oil. Fill the muffin cups with the mixture, about 2/3 way full. Then place the muffin cups in the air fryer tray or basket.

STEP 3

Set the air fryer timer for 13 minutes at 340 degrees F. serve, and enjoy!

Ranchero Breakfast

Prep Time: 6 mins Cook Time: 6 mins Total Time: 12 mins Servings: 2

INGREDIENTS

2 large gluten free flour tortillas

2 servings Tofu Scramble

2 fresh jalapeños, stemmed and sliced

1/2 cup+ Classic Ranchero Sauce

2 small corn tortillas

3/4 avocado, peeled and sliced

1/3 cup cooked pinto beans

DIRECTIONS

STEP 1

Place large tortillas on clean prep surface. Arrange crunchwraps by stacking ingredients in this order: tofu scramble, jalapeño slices, Ranchero Sauce, smaller corn tortillas, sliced avocado, and pinto beans. Put additional ranchero sauce as desired.

STEP 2

Fold large tortilla around fillings and seal completely.

STEP 3

Cook each Crunchwrap in the air fryer for 5 minutes at 360°F.

STEP 4

Pan fry in dry pan on a medium low heat for a few minutes on each side until golden brown.

Cornbread with agave butter

Prep Time: 6 mins Cook Time: 30 mins Total Time: 36 mins Servings: 2

INGREDIENTS

3/4 cup fine grind yellow cornmeal

1/2 cup sorghum flour

1/4 cup tapioca starch

1/4 cup granulated sugar

2 teaspoons baking powder

1/2 teaspoon xanthan gum

1/4 teaspoon fine sea salt

1 cup plain soymilk

3 tablespoons olive oil

2 teaspoons fresh minced rosemary

1/2 cup vegan butter, softened

Agave nectar, as needed

DIRECTIONS

STEP 1

Spray ramekins with cooking spray.

STEP 2

Mix together the cornmeal, sorghum flour, baking powder, tapioca starch, sugar, xanthan gum, and salt in a large bowl. Add the soymilk, olive oil and rosemary to the flour mixture, whisking until well combined.

STEP 3

Scoop the batter into the ramekins. Bake in the air fryer for 20 to 30 at 330 degrees f, until the toothpick inserted in the middle comes out clean or lightly browned on top.

STEP 4

Mix together butter and 2 tablespoon agave in a small bowl, until smooth

STEP 5

Remove the cornbread from air fryer and set aside to cool. Serve with a side of agave butter.

CHAPTER TWO

LUNCH & DINNER

Cajun French Fry with Mushroom Gravy

Prep Time: 25 mins Cook Time: 10 mins Total Time: 35 mins Servings: 4

INGREDIENTS

For French fry:

4 medium Idaho russet potatoes cut in half, and into planks

1/4 teaspoon granulated garlic

1/4 teaspoon ground black pepper

6 cups boiling water

For Mushroom Gravy:

1 tablespoon olive oil or water

1 tablespoon tapioca starch

3 cups chopped mushrooms

1/2 cup water

2 teaspoon soy sauce

2 teaspoon vegan Worcestershire sauce

Sandwich Options:

Fresh loaf of French or Italian bread

Vegan mayo

Lettuce

Sliced tomatoes

Tabasco or any favorite hot sauce

DIRECTIONS

Make the French Fries

STEP 1

Bring water to a boil in tea kettle, place the cut fries in a saucepan and then pour the boiled water over the fries, covering them. Let the fries soak in the hot water for about 15 minutes, then pour into a strainer on the sink. Once dry, toss the fries in the olive oil, Cajun seasoning, paprika, salt, garlic and black pepper.

STEP 2

Put the potato mixture in the air fryer basket and cook at 340°F for 10 minutes. Shake the basket half way through.

STEP 3

Increase the heat to 380°F and cook for 5 minutes, shake the basket and lastly, cook for more 5 minutes.

Make the Mushroom Gravy

STEP 1

While the potatoes are cooking, heat 1 tablespoon olive oil in a skillet on medium heat. Once hot, add mushrooms and sauté until they start to release their juices. Stir in soy sauce and Worcestershire sauce and cook for 2 minutes.

STEP 2

Add water and stir in the tapioca starch. Increase the heat to medium-high and cook until it thickens.

STEP 3

Assemble the Sandwich:

Cut the bread in half lengthwise. Toast the bread, spread vegan mayo or hot sauce on it, then dress with lettuce, tomato, and mayo.

STEP 4

Spread the mushroom mixture on top of the fried fries on the bottom piece of bread. Put the top piece of bread on top and enjoy!

Vegetarian Momos

Prep Time: 22 mins Cook Time: 15 mins Total Time: 37 mins Servings: 4

INGREDIENTS

1/4 cup chopped green onions

1 teaspoon soy sauce

16 wonton wrappers

1 tablespoon vegetable oil

3/4 cup shredded cabbage

3/4 cup shredded carrots

1/4 cup water or more

Cooking spray

DIRECTIONS

STEP 1

In a skillet, heat vegetable oil on a medium-high heat. Add carrots, cabbage and cook, stirring occasionally until softened, 4 minutes. Add green onion, cook for 3 minutes.

STEP 2

Drop skillet from heat and stir soy sauce into carrot/cabbage mixture. Let it cool for 10 minutes.

STEP 3

Preheat air fryer to 325°F (165°C).

STEP 4

Spoon 1 tablespoon carrot/cabbage mixture into the center of each wonton wrapper. Fold wrapper around the filling to form desired shape. Seal edges with water, if needed.

STEP 5

Spray vegetable momos with cooking spray and arrange them in the air fryer basket, working in batches.

STEP 6

Cook in air fryer for 5 minutes. Flip and cook until golden brown and crispy, about 5 minutes.

Veggie Balls

Prep Time: 4 mins Cook Time: 12 mins Total Time: 16 mins Servings: 4

INGREDIENTS

200 g Cauliflower

1/2 Cup Desiccated Coconut

2 teaspoon Garlic Puree

1 teaspoon Chives

100 g Sweet Potato

70 g Carrot

90 g Parsnips

2 teaspoon Oregano

1 teaspoon Paprika

1 teaspoon Mixed Spice

1 Cup Gluten Free Oats

Salt & Pepper

DIRECTIONS

STEP 1

Place cooked vegetables into a clean tea towel, squeeze out excess water.Put them in a clean mixing bowl and add seasoning. Mix thoroughly and roll into medium sized balls.

STEP 2

Put them in the fridge for 3 hours to firm up a bit.

STEP 3

Add together coconut and gluten free oats in a blender and whizz until it looks like rough flour. Pour into a bowl.

STEP 4

Dip the veggie balls in the mixture and then arrange them on the grill pan in the air fryer.

STEP 5

Cook at 200c/400f for 10 minutes. Roll over and cook for more 2 minutes. Serve.

Special Vegetable Noodles

Prep Time: 3 mins Cook Time: 6 mins Total Time: 9 mins Servings: 1

INGREDIENTS

2 spiralizable vegetables: Zucchini or sweet potatoes

DIRECTIONS

STEP 1

Using a spiral slicer, make noodles out of sweet potatoes or zucchini. Set the air fryer to 350°F and cook the noodles, stirring regularly, for 6 minutes.

STEP 2

When the noodles are springy and yet al dente, remove them. Toss with a sauce of your choice.

Sweet and Spicy Tofu

Prep Time 30 mins Cook Time 12 mins Total Time: 42 mins Servings: 2

INGREDIENTS

For The Tofu:

1 14 oz. Pack of Extra Firm Tofu

1/4 Cup Corn Starch

1/2 teaspoon Paprika

1 teaspoon Salt

1/2 teaspoon Onion Powder

For the Sweet and Spicy Sauce:

3 tablespoon Soy Sauce

1/2 tablespoon Sesame Oil

2 tablespoon Olive Oil

2 Cloves Garlic Minced

1 tablespoon Garlic Chili Sauce

DIRECTIONS

STEP 1

Preheat Air Fryer to 375 Degrees.

STEP 2

Slice Tofu into 8 pieces. Place them on a cutting board that is lined with paper towel. Place a paper towel on top of it and then put a heavy pan on it (you can use a Tofu press if you have one).

STEP 3

Cut each tofu into 8 pieces. Put them into ziplock bag. Add cornstarch into bag. Add Paprika, Salt and Onion Powder into bag and shake to evenly coat the Tofu.

STEP 4

Cook in Air Fryer for 11-12 minutes.

STEP 5

Meanwhile, add together Soy Sauce, Sesame Oil, Olive Oil, brown sugar and Garlic Chili Paste. Toss the Tofu in the sauce once it's been cooked.

STEP 6

Serve immediately.

Palatable Crab Cakes

Prep Time: 8 mins Cook Time: 20 mins Total Time: 30 mins Servings: 4

INGREDIENTS

1 16 ounce garbanzo beans

2 14 ounce can hearts of palm drained and rinsed

4 tablespoons garbanzo liquid

1 1/2 teaspoons vegan Worcestershire sauce

1 1/2 teaspoons Old Bay Seasoning

1 teaspoon garlic powder

2 teaspoons mustard

1/4 cup vegan mayonnaise

1 tablespoon fresh lemon juice

1/2 cup green onions

1/2 tablespoon kelp seasoning

1 tablespoon dried parsley

1 cup of panko breadcrumbs (more for breading)

DIRECTIONS

STEP 1

Put the beans and artichokes to a clean bowl and shred them up with the back of a fork. Set aside.

STEP 2

Wisk the reserved garbanzo bean liquid in a bowl until frothy. Add the lemon juice, mayo, Worcestershire sauce, mustard and all the dry ingredients. Mix well.

STEP 3

Add the breadcrumbs, green onions, hearts of palm and bean mixture. Mix to combine. Put in the freezer for 20 minutes or more.

STEP 4

Put breadcrumbs on a clean plate to coat patties. Put some of the mixture on your palm and roll into a ball. Pat it into a patty shape.

STEP 5

Coat the patty with the breadcrumbs on both side and place it in the air fryer basket.

STEP 6

Set the air fryer to 380 degrees and cook for 10 minutes, flip patty over after 5 minutes. Serve with any sauce of your choice.

Buffalo Cauliflower

Prep Time: 3 mins Cook Time: 20 mins Total Time: 23 mins Servings: 4

INGREDIENTS

1 large head cauliflower

1 cup unbleached all-purpose flour

1/4 teaspoon chili powder

2 tablespoons nondairy butter

1/2 cup Original Cayenne Pepper Sauce

1/4 teaspoon paprika

1/4 teaspoon dried chipotle chile flakes

1 cup soy milk

Canola oil spray

1 teaspoon vegan chicken bouillon granules

1/4 teaspoon cayenne pepper

2 cloves garlic, minced

DIRECTIONS

STEP 1

Cauliflower should be cut into small pieces, rinsed and drained.

STEP 2

In a large mixing bowl, combine the flour, cayenne, bouillon granules, chili powder, paprika, and chipotle flakes. Slowly pour in the milk, stirring constantly, until you have a thick batter.

STEP 3

Preheat the air fryer to 380 degrees F for 10 minutes after spraying some canola oil into the basket.

STEP 4

Toss the cauliflower in the batter while the air fryer is heating up. Fill the air fryer basket with battered cauliflower. Cook for 20 minutes at 390°F. Turn the cauliflower pieces with tongs after 10 minutes.

STEP 5

In a small saucepan over medium high heat, melt the butter, hot sauce, and garlic. Bring the mixture to a boil, then reduce to a low heat and cover.

STEP 6

Transfer the cauliflower to a clean large mixing bowl once it's done cooking. Toss the cauliflower with tongs after pouring the sauce over it. Serve right away.

Crispy BBQ Soy Curls

Prep Time: 13 mins Cook Time: 8 mins Total Time: 21 mins Servings: 2

INGREDIENTS

1 cup warm water

1 teaspoon vegetarian Better Than Bouillon

1 cup Soy Curls

1/4 cup BBQ sauce

1 teaspoon canola oil divided

DIRECTIONS

STEP 1

Soak Soy Curls and Bouillon for 10 minutes in a bowl of water. Drain in a sieve and squeeze off any excess liquid. Pull apart the hydrated Curls into shreds and place them in a mixing dish.

STEP 2

Air fried the Soy Curls at 400 degrees for 3 minutes.

STEP 3

Remove the Curls from the air fryer, place them in a mixing dish, and toss with the BBQ sauce, stirring to coat evenly.

STEP 4

Return to the air fryer and cook for 5 minutes at 400 degrees, shaking the pan twice.

Vegetarian Falafel

Prep Time: 13 mins Cook Time: 30 mins Total Time: 43 mins Servings: 4

INGREDIENTS

1 can chickpeas, rinsed and drained

1 small yellow onion, quartered

1/2 teaspoon kosher salt

1/8 teaspoon crushed red pepper flakes

3 cloves garlic, chopped

1/3 cup chopped parsley

1/3 cup chopped cilantro

1/3 cup chopped scallions

1 teaspoon cumin

1 teaspoon baking powder

4 tablespoons all-purpose flour (more for dusting)

Olive oil spray

Hummus, pita, sliced red onion, sliced tomatoes (optional)

DIRECTIONS

STEP 1

Use a paper towel to dry chickpeas.

STEP 2

Add the onions and garlic in the food processor bowl. Add the cumin, scallions, cilantro, parsley, salt, and red pepper flakes. Process about 60 seconds until blended, then add the chickpeas and pulse 3 times until well blended, but not pureed.

STEP 3

Add in the baking powder and the flour, scape the sides of the processor bowl with a clean spatula and pulse 2 times.

STEP 4

Pour into a bowl, cover and refrigerate for 3 hours.

STEP 5

Roll the falafel mixture into 12 balls

STEP 6

Preheat air fryer 350F. Spray the falafel with olive oil. Cook in batches for 14 minutes, until golden brown, flipping halfway. Enjoy

Chickpea Tacos

Prep Time: 4 mins Cook Time: 12 mins Total Time: 16 mins Servings: 4

INGREDIENTS

14 oz. tin chickpeas rinsed, drained and dried

2 teaspoon olive oil

1/2 teaspoon smoked paprika

1/2 ground cumin

Salt

8 small corn tortillas

Taco toppings

Radishes thinly sliced

Avocado

Shredded cabbage

Cranberries

Coconut yoghurt

Lime

DIRECTIONS

STEP 1

Preheat air fryer to 390F / 200C.

STEP 2

Add all the ingredients in a clean mixing bowl and mix.

STEP 3

Place the chickpeas in to the air fryer basket. Cook for approximately 15 minutes, turning halfway through.

STEP 4

Arrange tacos on a plate and serve with limes and coconut yoghurt.

Red Bean-Chipotle Burgers

Prep Time: 16 mins Cook Time: 25 mins Total Time: 41 mins Servings: 6

INGREDIENTS

1 small size onion, peeled and cut into quarters

1 clove garlic

1-3 teaspoons chopped canned chipotles OR hot smoked paprika, to taste

2 tablespoons whole wheat flour

1 16 oz. can kidney beans, drained and rinsed

1/2 cup quick oats or old fashioned, uncooked

1/2 cup cooked brown rice

1 tablespoon tomato paste

1/2 teaspoon salt (optional for salt-free diets)

1/2 teaspoon oregano

1/2 teaspoon thyme

DIRECTIONS

STEP 1

Preheat air fryer to 390 F.

STEP 2

Put garlic and onion into a food processor and pulse. Put the beans and process until coarsely chopped. Add the remaining ingredients and process until it is well blended but not to a paste.

STEP 3

Line a cookie sheet with parchment paper. Scoop the burger mixture onto the baking sheet using 1/3 cup measurement; use a spoon to smoothing it into six patties.

STEP 4

Place them into the air fryer and cook for 8 minutes. Flip burgers over and re-arrange from top to bottom if using a rack. Cook for 5-8 more minutes, until burgers are firm and crispy outside. Do not overcook.

STEP 5

Serve immediately with accompaniments.

Orange Tofu

Prep Time: 4 mins Cook Time: 15 mins Total Time: 20 mins Servings: 2

INGREDIENTS

14 oz. block firm tofu, organic non-GMO

1 tablespoon tapioca

Sea salt to taste

Orange Glaze:

4 tablespoon orange juice

3 tablespoon apple cider vinegar

2 tablespoon almond butter, cashew or walnut

4 inch orange peel

2 tablespoon soy sauce

1 pinch red pepper flakes

DIRECTIONS

STEP 1

To begin, drain the tofu and pat it dry with a tea towel.

STEP 2

Place a heavy pan on top and leave to press for several hours at room temperature. Tear the tofu into uneven 1.5-inch pieces with your hands. Toss with the tapioca and a bit of salt to coat.

STEP 3

Arrange the tofu in the air fryer tray so that they don't touch. Air fried for 14 minutes at 400 degrees F, tossing halfway through; do not overcook the tofu. When the timer goes off, remove the item.

Make the Orange Sauce:

STEP 1

Whisk together all of the ingredients until smooth. Transfer to a skillet and cook over medium heat for 2 minutes, or until thick and sticky.

STEP 2

Toss the cooked tofu in the orange sauce to cover it evenly. Serve with chives, scallions, and sesame seeds on top of the noodles.

Portobello Mushroom

Prep Time: 6 mins Cook Time: 7 mins Total Time: 13 mins Servings: 2

INGREDIENTS

1/4 cup balsamic vinegar

1/4 cup olive oil

2 Portobello mushroom caps stems removed

1/4 cup basil pesto

2 tablespoon lemon juice

1 tablespoon Dijon mustard

1/2 teaspoon Kosher salt

2 tablespoon mayo we used Just Mayo

DIRECTIONS

STEP 1

To make marinade, whisk together balsamic vinegar, olive oil, lemon juice, mustard, and salt in a small bowl.

STEP 2

Take out the stems from mushroom caps and clean with a damp paper towel. Place mushrooms in a re-sealable plastic bag. Pour in marinade, sea and toss to coat. Let marinate for at 30 minutes or more, turning halfway through.

STEP 3

Spray oil into the air fryer to prevent sticking. Put Portobello into the air fryer basket and cook at 370 degrees for 7 minutes.

STEP 4

Meanwhile, prepare toppings of choice. Combine pesto and mayonnaise, sauté spinach, and slice tomatoes and red onions.

STEP 5

Once cook time is complete, remove mushrooms and let sit on separate plate for some minutes.

Oil-Free Fries

Prep Time: 3 mins Cook Time: 30 mins Total Time: 33 mins Servings: 1

INGREDIENTS

3 medium red potatoes

1 teaspoon garlic powder

1/4 teaspoon basil

1 teaspoon onion powder

1/4 teaspoon chili powder

1/4 teaspoon paprika

Salt to taste

DIRECTIONS

STEP 1

Peel and rinse potatoes. Slice the potatoes.

STEP 2

Toss the fries with the other ingredients.

STEP 3

Transfer the fries into the air fryer basket. Fry at 380 degrees for 27-30 minutes. Stir every 5-10 minutes. Dip in ketchup and enjoy.

Stuffed peppers with veggie sausage & rice

Prep Time: 11 mins Cook Time: 14 mins Total Time: 25 mins Servings: 2

INGREDIENTS

1 teaspoon organic canola oil

1 veggie sausage sliced

1/2 cup chopped yellow onion

2 cloves garlic minced

1 cup cooked brown rice or white

1/4 cup marinara

1/4 teaspoon dried oregano

1/4 teaspoon dried basil

1/4 teaspoon granulated onion

Pinch salt

Dash pepper

2 Tablespoons shredded non-dairy cheese Optional

1 large red bell pepper

DIRECTIONS

STEP 1

In a large skillet, heat the oil over medium heat. Toss in the sausage slices in the skillet. Break apart the sausage in the pan with a spatula as it cooks.

STEP 2

Add onions and garlic once the sausage has browned. Sauté for a few minutes, until the mixture is fragrant. Add the cooked rice, marinara, granulated onion, dried oregano, dried basil, pinch of salt, and a pinch of pepper. Use the spatula to stir everything together. Drop the pan from the heat and set it aside.

STEP 3

Using a sharp knife, cut the bell pepper in half lengthwise. Remove the seeds and white membrane from inside the pepper halves with your fingers.

STEP 4

Place the pepper halves, empty side down, in the air fryer. Cook for 7 minutes at 370°F in an air fryer.

STEP 5

When the timer goes off, take the pepper halves from the air fryer and use a spoon to fill them with the rice mixture. Place the full halves, rice side up, back into the air fryer. Cook for 7 minutes at 370°F in an air fryer.

STEP 6

After 4 minutes, top each pepper with a spoonful of shredded non-dairy cheese. Continue to heat until all of the cheese has melted.

STEP 7

Remove the peppers from the air fryer and toss with vegetables or salad right away.

CHAPTER THREE

SIDES & SNACKS

Fried Kale Chips

Prep time: 3 mins Cook time: 20 mins Total time: 23 mins Servings: 4

INGREDIENTS

1 bunch kale, stemmed, washed and spun - torn into small size pieces

1 tablespoon olive oil

1-2 tablespoon za'atar seasoning

1/2 - 1 teaspoon sea salt

DIRECTIONS

STEP 1

Place kale into a large mixing bowl and drizzle with olive oil.

STEP 2

Lightly massage the olive oil into the kale with your hands, until well coated. Stir in the seasonings until everything is fully combined.

STEP 3

In batches, place kale in the air fryer basket, set to 180 degrees C for 20 minutes.

Gluten-free Crispy potato

Prep Time: 3 mins Cook Time: 8 mins Total Time: 11 mins Servings: 4

INGREDIENTS

2 1/2 Cups Peeled, Shredded White Potato

1/2 Cup Minced Sweet Onion

3 tablespoon Arrowroot Starch

1 Prepared Bob's Red Mill Egg Replacement

1/2 teaspoon Smoked Paprika (optional)

1/4 teaspoon Black Pepper (optional)

Applesauce (to serve)

DIRECTIONS

STEP 1

Preheat air fryer to 350°F (175 degrees C).

STEP 2

Mix together the potato, onion, starch, and prepared egg in a clean large bowl. Remove 2 tablespoons of the mixture and form a thick disc.

STEP 3

Place in the air fryer (do in batches). Keep even space in the air fryer basket for perfect browning. Air fry for 5 minutes, flip and air fry for another 3 minutes until golden brown and crisp.

Avocado Fries

Prep Time: 9 mins Cook Time: 10 mins Total Time: 19 mins Servings: 4

INGREDIENTS

1/2 cup panko breadcrumbs

1/2 teaspoon salt

1 Haas avocado, peeled and sliced

Aquafaba from 115 oz can white beans

DIRECTIONS

STEP 1

In a clean shallow bowl, toss together the panko and salt. Pour the aquafaba into another clean bowl.

STEP 2

Dip the avocado slices in the aquafaba and then in the panko to have a nice even coating.

STEP 3

Arrange the avocado slices in a single layer in air fryer basket. Do not overlap. Air fry at 390 degrees F for 10 minutes, shaking the basket after 5 minutes.

STEP 4

Serve with your favorite dipping sauce!

Crispy Plantains

INGREDIENTS

1 plantain

3/4 teaspoon oil

Salt to taste

DIRECTIONS

STEP 1

Preheat the air fryer to 360 F.

STEP 2

Peel the plantain, slice it and add to a clean bowl.

STEP 3

Gently mix in drizzle with oil and salt until plantains are coated on both sides.

STEP 4

Place half of the plantain slices in a single layer in the air fryer basket. Cook for 10 minutes, flipping the plantain halfway through. Serve warm.

Baked Potato

Prep Time: 4 mins Cook Time: 30 mins Total Time: 34 mins Servings: 4

INGREDIENTS

4 Russet potatoes scrubbed clean and dried

2 teaspoons olive oil

1 teaspoon kosher salt

DIRECTIONS

STEP 1

Prick each potato with a sharp knife. Brush the potatoes with olive oil and sprinkle with some salt. Place the potatoes in the air fryer basket, leaving enough room between them for air to flow while they cook.

STEP 2

Set the air fryer to 390 degrees F for 30 minutes.

STEP 3

When its time, open the air fryer and press on the sides of the potato.

STEP 4

Split open each potatoes with a knife and add your favorite toppings.

Bow Tie Pasta Chips

Prep Time: 27 mins Cook Time: 10 mins Total Time: 37 mins Servings: 2

INGREDIENTS

2 c dry whole wheat bow tie pasta

1 tablespoon olive oil

1 tablespoon nutritional yeast

1 1/2 teaspoon Italian Seasoning Blend

1/2 teaspoon salt

DIRECTIONS

STEP 1

Cook the pasta for half the amount of time specified on the package. Drained the pasta and toss with olive oil, nutritional yeast, Italian seasoning and salt.

STEP 2

Cook for 5 minutes at 380°F (200°C) in the air fryer basket using roughly half of the mixture. Shake the basket and Cook for another 4 to 5 minutes, or until crispy.

Grilled Tomatoes

Prep Time: 1 min Cook Time: 13 mins Total Time: 14 mins Servings: 2

INGREDIENTS

3 Medium Beefcake Tomatoes

1 teaspoon Oregano

Salt & Pepper

DIRECTIONS

STEP 1

Cut the tomatoes in half. Place the tomatoes on top of the air fryer grill pan and Sprinkle with salt, pepper and oregano.

STEP 2

Cook for 8 minutes at 180c/360f and then for 5 minutes more at 160c/320f so that it can cook in the middle. Serve.

Portobello Mushroom Pizzas with Hummus

Prep Time: 13 mins Cook Time: 10 mins Total Time: 23 mins Servings: 4

INGREDIENTS

4 large portobello mushrooms

3 ounces zucchini shredded, chopped

2 tablespoons sweet red pepper diced

4 olives kalamata olives sliced

1 teaspoon dried basil

Balsamic vinegar

Salt and black pepper

4 tablespoons oil-free pasta sauce

1 clove garlic minced

1/2 cups hummus

Fresh basil leaves

DIRECTIONS

STEP 1

Wash the portobellos very well. Cut the stems and remove the gills. Pat the insides dry and spray both sides with balsamic vinegar. Sprinkle inside with salt and pepper.

STEP 2

Spread 1 tablespoon of pasta sauce inside each mushroom and sprinkle with garlic.

STEP 3

Preheat the Air Fryer to 330 degrees F. In a single layer, arrange as many mushrooms as will fit. Air Fry for 3 minutes (you may need to do this in batches depending on the size of air fryer).

STEP 4

Remove mushrooms and top each one with zucchini, peppers, and olives and sprinkle with dried basil and salt and pepper. Return to the Air Fryer and air fry for 3 minutes.

STEP 5

Check mushrooms and rearrange if using a rack. Transfer back to the Air Fryer for another 3 minutes.

STEP 6

Put on a plate, drizzle with hummus and sprinkle with basil.

Baked Apple

Prep Time: 11 mins Cook Time: 20 mins Total Time: 31 mins Servings: 2

INGREDIENTS

1 medium apple

2 tablespoon raisins

1/4 teaspoon nutmeg

1/4 teaspoon cinnamon

1 1/4 teaspoons light margarine, melted

2 tablespoon chopped walnuts

1/4 cup water

DIRECTIONS

STEP1

Preheat air fryer to 350° F.

STEP 2

Cut the apple in half around the middle and spoon out the flesh. Place the apple in air fryer pan.

STEP 3

In a small mixing dish, combine margarine, nutmeg, cinnamon, walnuts, and raisins.

STEP 4

Using a spoon put the mixture into the apple halves' centers.

STEP 5

Put water in the pan and Bake for 20 minutes.

Crispy Tangy Reuben Rolls

Prep Time: 14 mins Cook Time: 10 mins Total Time: 24 mins Servings:12

INGREDIENTS

1 (20 ounce) can jackfruit, drained

1/3 cup oil free Vegan Thousand Island Dressing

2 large dill pickles, chopped

12-14 vegan wonton wrappers

1 small sweet onion, peeled and diced

2 cloves garlic, peeled and minced

6-7 thin slices vegan Swiss cheese, optional

DIRECTIONS

STEP 1

Shred jackfruit with fork. Toss in the Vegan Thousand Island Dressing and set aside to marinate.

STEP 2

Over medium heat, cook onion and garlic in a saucepan with a little water. Remove the pan from the heat and stir in the jackfruit mixture.

STEP 3

Arrange a wrap in a diamond shape. In the bottom corner, place 2 teaspoons of the jackfruit mixture. Add a half-slice of cheese and a spoonful of pickles to the mix. Fold each fold and brush with pickle juice.

STEP 4

Arrange Crispy Tangy Reuben Rolls in a single layer on a baking sheet and bake for 6 minutes at 360 degrees F.

STEP 5

Remove and shake basket. Cook for another 3 minutes, or until golden brown and crisp.

STEP 6

Serve warm with Vegan Thousand Island Dressing.

CHAPTER FOUR

DESSERTS

Brownies

Prep Time: 7 mins Cook Time: 18 mins Total Time: 25 mins Servings: 2

INGREDIENTS

1/2 cup granulated sugar

1/3 cup cocoa powder

1/4 cup all-purpose flour

1/4 teaspoon baking powder

Pinch kosher salt

1/4 cup butter, melted and cooled slightly

1 large egg

DIRECTIONS

STEP 1

Use cooking spray to grease a 6 inch round cake pan.

Step 2

Add sugar, cocoa powder, flour, baking powder, salt in a bowl and mix.

Step 3

In another bowl, mix melted butter and egg together.

STEP 4

Mix the mixture in the first bowl and the second bowl together to form a batter. Mix thoroughly.

STEP 5

Pour the brownie batter into the prepared pan and use spoon to smoothing the top.

STEP 6

Cook in the air fryer at 350f for 18 minutes. Leave to cool for about 10 minutes and slice.

Chocolate Chip Cookies

Prep Time: 4 mins Cook Time: 8 mins Total Time: 12 mins Servings: 8

INGREDIENTS

8 oz. (200g) cookie dough mix

1/8 cup chocolate chips optional

Parchment paper

DIRECTIONS

STEP 1

Preheat air fryer to 350F / 180C.

STEP 2

Make cookie dough according to instructions on the package and add in any extras you want.

STEP 3

Split the dough into 8 small cookies.

STEP 4

Place parchment paper in the air fryer basket, then place cookies on top, leaving space between them. Optional: add the extra chocolate chips to the cookies.

STEP 5

Bake for 5 minutes, remove and let it cool on a rack.

Easy Churros

Prep Time: 8 mins Cook Time: 5 mins Total Time: 13 mins Servings: 4

INGREDIENTS

1 cup (250mL) water

1/4 teaspoon salt

1 tablespoon sugar

1/2 cup (113g) butter

1 cup (120g) all-purpose flour

4 eggs

Sifted powdered sugar and cinnamon

DIRECTIONS

STEP 1

Mix the butter, water, salt and sugar in a pan, bring to a boil, stirring constantly.

STEP 2

Add the flour and continue to mix. Drop from heat and continue to mix until smooth. Add the eggs one after the other, mix until thoroughly. Set aside to cool.

STEP 3

Preheat Air Fryer to 400F/200C.

STEP 4

Transfer dough into a cake decorator bag and add a 1/2-inch star tip.

STEP 5

Make sticks that are 4 inches in length by pushing the dough out of the bag onto a parchment paper.

STEP 6

Transfer straight to the air fryer. If the dough is too soft to handle, put it in the fridge for 20 minutes to firm up. Using cooking spray, coat the air fryer basket.

STEP 7

Add 8-10 churros in air fryer basket. Spray with oil. Cook at 400F/200C for 5 minutes on French settings.

STEP 8

Once done, roll in cinnamon sugar mixture or regular sugar.

Fried Oreos

Prep Time: 10 mins Cook Time: 4 mins Total Time: 14 mins Servings: 9

INGREDIENTS

9 Oreo cookies

1 crescent sheet roll

DIRECTIONS

STEP 1

Preheat Air Fryer to 360F/182C.

STEP 2

Open the crescent roll tube and spread the dough out on a work surface in a full sheet. Make 9 equal squares by lining them up and cutting them out.

STEP 3

Put 1 Oreo cookie in each dough square and wrap them up.

STEP 4

Cook the dough-wrapped cookies for 4 minutes in a fryer basket. Turn and toss Halfway through.

Blueberry Hand Pies

Prep Time: 12 mins Cook Time: 12 mins Total Time: 24 mins Servings: 8

INGREDIENTS

1 cup (128g) blueberries

2.5 tablespoon caster sugar

1 teaspoon lemon juice

1 pinch salt

14 ounces (320g) refrigerated pie crust

Water

Vanilla sugar to sprinkle on top (optional)

DIRECTIONS

STEP 1

Mix the blueberries, sugar, lemon juice, and salt together in a clean medium bowl.

STEP 2

Spread out the piecrusts and cut out 6-8 (4-inch) circles. Put about 1 tablespoon of the blueberry filling in the middle of each circle.

STEP 3

Use water to moisten the edges of dough, and roll the dough over the filling to make a half moon shape. Gently crimp the edges of the piecrust together with a fork. Slice 3 slits on the top of the pies.

STEP 4

Spray the pies with cooking spray and sprinkle with some vanilla sugar (optional).

Preheat air fryer to 350F / 170C.

STEP 5

Put 3-4 hand pies in the air fryer basket in a single layer and cook for 10-12 minutes. Remove the pies and set aside to cool for 10 minutes before serving.

Caramel Apple Donuts

Prep Time: 15 mins Cook Time: 9 mins Total Time: 24 mins Servings: 8

INGREDIENTS

1 apple diced small

1/8 teaspoon apple pie spice

2 tablespoons caramel sauce

1 roll of pizza dough

3 tablespoons of sugar

1 teaspoon cinnamon

3 tablespoons melted butter

DIRECTIONS

STEP 1

Put diced apple into a non-stick saucepan and cook for on a low heat, stirring frequently for about 5 minutes or until soft. Add and stir in the apple pie spice and caramel sauce and turn off the heat.

STEP 2

Roll out pizza dough and cut into 6-inch x 2-inch strips.

STEP 3

Spoon a line of the caramel apple mixture down the center of each donut strip.

STEP 4

Join the edges of each doughnut strip and seal them together, then curl the ends of each piece to form a round and seal it.

STEP 5

Preheat air fryer to 350F / 180C and spray the basket with olive oil spray.

STEP 6

Cook for 7- 9 minutes, shaking halfway through.

STEP 7

Melt butter in a bowl and combine sugar and cinnamon in another bowl. Dip donuts first into the butter, then coat with cinnamon sugar before serving.

Nutella Smores

Prep Time: 4 mins Cook Time: 5 mins Total Time: 9 mins Servings: 4

INGREDIENTS

4 graham crackers cut in half

4 jumbo marshmallows

Strawberries and Raspberries

4 teaspoon of Nutella

DIRECTIONS

STEP 1

Preheat air fryer to 340 F / 170 C and Place 4 graham cracker halves in the air fryer basket.

STEP 2

Place 1 marshmallow on top of each cracker half and Cook for 5 minutes, until marshmallow is golden. Put the berries and the Nutella.

STEP 3

Top each with a graham cracker half. Serve and enjoy!

Gluten-Free Chocolate Cake

**Prep Time: 12 mins Cook Time: 55 mins Total Time: 1 hr 7 mins
Servings: 10**

INGREDIENTS

3 large eggs

1 cup (128g) almond flour

2/3 cup (85g) sugar

1/3 cup (78ml) heavy cream

1/4 cup (59ml) coconut oil melted

1/4 cup (32g) unsweetened cocoa powder

1 teaspoon baking powder

1/2 teaspoon orange zest

1/8 cup (16g) chopped walnuts

1/8 cup (16g) chopped pecans

Unsalted butter

DIRECTIONS

STEP 1

Butter the bottom of a 7-inch round baking pan and line it with parchment paper.

STEP 2

Add all the ingredients in a large mixing bowl and mix on medium speed with a hand mixer until the batter is frothy and light. To maintain the air in the batter, gently incorporate the nuts into the batter.

STEP 3

Cover the cake batter with aluminum foil and place it in the pan. Cook for 45 minutes at 330 degrees F in an air fryer basket.

STEP 4

Cook for a further 12-15 minutes after removing the foil, or until a toothpick inserted in the center comes out clean.

STEP 5

Place the pan on a cooling rack for 10 minutes after removing it from the air fryer. After that, take the cake out of the pan and set it aside to cool for about 20 minutes. Slice and serve.

Spiced Apples

Prep Time: 6 mins Cook Time: 10 mins Total Time: 16 mins Servings: 4

INGREDIENTS

4 small apples, sliced

2 tablespoons coconut oil

2 tablespoons sugar*

1 teaspoon apple pie spice

DIRECTIONS

STEP 1

Place the apples in a mixing bowl. Sprinkle with sugar and apple pie spice after drizzling with coconut oil. Put the apples in the mixture to coat them.

STEP 2

Place the apples in an air fryer pan before placing them in the basket. Cook for 10 minutes at 350°F. Cook for an additional 3-5 minutes if the apples are not soft after being pierced with a knife. Serve with a scoop of ice cream on the side.

Fried Banana S'mores

Prep Time: 12 mins Cook Time: 6 mins Total Time: 18 mins Servings: 4

INGREDIENTS

4 bananas

3 tablespoons graham cracker cereal

3 tablespoons mini semi-sweet chocolate chips

3 tablespoons mini marshmallows

3 tablespoons mini peanut butter chips

DIRECTIONS

STEP 1

Preheat the air fryer to 400ºF.

STEP 2

Cut lengthwise into the unpeeled bananas, but avoid cutting through the bottom of the peel. To make a pocket, open the banana.

STEP 3

Stuff chocolate chips, peanut butter chips, and marshmallows into each banana pocket. Graham cracker cereal should be pressed into the filling.

STEP 4

In the air fryer basket, arrange the bananas in an overlapping pattern to keep them upright and the filling facing up. Cook for 6 minutes in the air fryer, or until the banana is tender.

STEP 5

Set aside for a few minutes to cool before serving with a spoon to scoop out the contents.

CHAPTER FIVE

WEIGHT LOSS RECIPES

Mini Quiche Wedges

Prep time: 10 mins Cook time: 24 minutes Total Time: 34 minsServings:9

INGREDIENTS

100 g ready-made pie crust dough

1/2 tablespoon oil

1 egg

3 tablespoons whipping cream

40 g grated cheese

2 small pie moulds of 10 cm

Freshly ground pepper

Filling as desired

DIRECTIONS

STEP 1

Preheat the air fryer to 200°C.

STEP 2

Cut two 15-cm rounds out of the dough. Grease the molds with oil and press the dough into the bottoms and around the edges.

STEP 3

Combine the egg, cream, and cheese in a mixing bowl and season to taste with salt and pepper. Fill the molds with the mixture and the filling.

STEP 4

Put the molds in the basket and Slide the basket into the air fryer. Set the timer to 12 minutes at 350°F and bake the quiche until golden brown. It's possible to do it in batches.

STEP 5

Take the quiches out of the molds and cut each one into six wedges.

STEP 6

Warm the quiche slices before serving.

Ricotta Balls with Basil

Prep time: 15 mins Cook time: 16 mins Total Time: 1 mins Servings: 20

INGREDIENTS

8 oz. ricotta

2 tablespoons flour

1 tablespoon chives, finely chopped

3 slices of stale white bread

1 egg, separated

Freshly ground pepper

1 cup fresh chopped basil

DIRECTIONS

STEP 1

In a clean basin, combine the ricotta, flour, egg yolk, 1 teaspoon salt, and freshly ground pepper. Stir in the basil, orange peel, and chives in a mixing bowl.

STEP 2

With damp hands, divide the mixture into 20 equal amounts and roll them into balls. Allow a few minutes for the balls to rest.

STEP 3

Grind the bread slices into fine breadcrumbs in a food processor and combine with the olive oil. Place the mixture in a serving dish. In a separate bowl, quickly beat the egg white.

STEP 4

Preheat the Air fryer to 395°F.

STEP 5

Drop the ricotta balls in the egg white and then in the breadcrumbs to coat them.

STEP 6

Place ten balls in the air fryer basket and place it in the air fryer. Set air fryer to 350°F and bake the balls for 8 minutes, or until golden brown. Organize your work in batches.

STEP 7

Serve and enjoy the ricotta balls.

Butternut Squash

Prep time: 5 mins Cook time: 20 mins Total Time: 25 mins Servings: 4

INGREDIENTS

4 cups Butternut squash - peeled and cut into cubes

1 tablespoon Extra virgin olive oil

1 tablespoon maple syrup

½ teaspoon salt

¼ teaspoon ground black pepper

sprigs fresh rosemary

DIRECTIONS

STEP1

Combine all of the ingredients in a large mixing basin and stir until well blended.

STEP 2

Coat the air fryer basket with nonstick cooking spray before using it to cook.

STEP 3

In the air frying basket, arrange the prepared butternut squash cubes in a single layer.

STEP 4

Cook for 20 minutes at 325 degrees, stirring halfway through.

Roasted Asian Broccoli

Prep Time: 12 mins Cook Time: 20 mins Total time: 32 mins Servings: 4

INGREDIENTS

1 Lb. Broccoli, Cut into florets

1 1/2 tablespoon Peanut oil

1 tablespoon Garlic, minced

Salt

2 tablespoon Reduced sodium soy sauce

2 teaspoon Honey (or agave)

2 teaspoon Sriracha

1 teaspoon Rice vinegar

1/3 Cup Roasted salted peanuts

Fresh lime juice (optional)

DIRECTIONS

STEP 1

In a mixing dish, combine the broccoli, peanut oil, and garlic; season with salt. Rub each one with your palm to ensure that the oil covers all of the broccoli florets.

STEP 2

Arrange the broccoli in a single layer in the wire basket of the air fryer and cook at 380 degrees for 17–20 minutes, stirring halfway through.

STEP 3

In a small microwave-safe bowl, combine the honey, soy sauce, sriracha, and rice vinegar and microwave for 17 seconds, or until the honey has melted.

STEP 4

Toss the cooked broccoli with the soy sauce mixture in a clean basin. Toss to coat and season with a pinch of salt to taste.

STEP 5

Toss in the peanuts and finish with a squeeze of lime (optional)

Greek Potatoes Mix

Prep Time: 6 mins Cook Time: 16 mins Total Time: 22 mins Servings: 4

INGREDIENTS

1 lb. (448g) Baby Gold Potatoes, quartered

1 tablespoon (15g) Lemon Juice

1/2 teaspoon Lemon Zest

1/2 teaspoon Dried Oregano

1 1/2 teaspoon Cavender's Greek Seasoning

1 tablespoon (16g) Olive Oil

1/4 teaspoon Black Pepper (optional)

DIRECTIONS

STEP 1

In a clean large mixing bowl, add the olive oil, lemon juice, and zest and mix. Set aside.

STEP 2

Rinse and quarter the potatoes before tossing with the oil and lemon juice mixture.

STEP 3

Transfer the potatoes to the air fryer basket with a spatula, leaving the remaining oil and lemon juice in the mixing bowl. Remove the bowl from the table. Air fry for 11 minutes at 390 degrees F.

STEP 4

When the potatoes are done, return them to the bowl containing the remaining oil and juice, along with the Greek spice, oregano, and black pepper. Toss to coat, then return the potatoes to the air fryer at 400°F for 5-8 minutes.

STEP 5

Combine the potatoes and chopped parsley in a large mixing bowl.

Cherry Tomato Salad

Prep Time: 4 mins Cook Time: 5 mins Total Time: 9 mins Servings: 4

INGREDIENTS

500 g Cherry Tomatoes

1 teaspoon Extra Virgin Olive Oil

1 teaspoon Dried Basil

Salt & Pepper

200 g Mozzarella Cheese Balls optional

Fresh Basil optional

DIRECTIONS

STEP 1

Half-cut the cherry tomatoes. Combine the cherry tomatoes, extra virgin olive oil, and dried basil in a mixing dish. With your hands, properly combine the ingredients and place them in the air fryer basket.

STEP 2

Cook at160°C/320°F and bake for 5 minutes.

STEP 3

Once the cherry tomatoes have warmed up, place them in a salad dish with shredded fresh basil and mini mozzarella cheese balls. Toss everything together and serve.

Roasted Beets

Prep Time: 11 mins Cook Time: 15 mins Total Time: 26 mins Servings: 4

INGREDIENTS

2 lbs. beets

1 1/2 teaspoon olive oil

1/8 teaspoon flaky salt {optional}

DIRECTIONS

STEP 1

Preheat the air fryer to 400 F.

STEP 2

Remove the beets' tops and root ends. Salads can be made with the leftovers. Using a knife, peel the skin from each beet and cut it into halves and quarters.

STEP 3

Drop the beets in a bowl with the olive oil. Toss to coat.

STEP 4

Spritz the air fryer basket with olive oil. Spread the beets around.

STEP 5

Cook at 400°F for 15 minutes, shaking every 8 minutes. Cook until the beets can be penetrated easily with a fork. Enjoy with a pinch of salt.

Potato Croquettes

Prep Time: 30 mins Cook Time: 8 mins Total Time: 38 mins Servings: 4

INGREDIENTS

300 g starchy potatoes, peeled and cubed

1 egg yolk

50 g Parmesan cheese, grated

2 tablespoons flour

Freshly ground pepper

Nutmeg

50 g bread crumbs

DIRECTIONS

STEP 1

In a pot of salted water, bring the potato to a boil for 15 minutes. Drain the potatoes and mash them. Allow the mashed potatoes to cool.

STEP 2

Whisk together the egg yolk, cheese, flour, and chives with the potato purée. Salt, pepper and nutmeg.

STEP 3

Preheat the air fryer to 200 degrees Celsius.

STEP 4

Add the bread crumbs and oil and toss until the mixture is loose and crumbly again.

STEP 5

Make 12 croquettes out of the potato purée and cover them with bread crumbs.

STEP 6

Place 6 croquettes in a fryer basket and place it in an air fryer. Set the timer for 4 minutes and fry until the potatoes are golden brown and crispy. Then repeat with the remaining croquettes.

Squash and Zucchini

Prep Time: 4 mins Cook Time: 15 mins Total Time: 19 mins Servings: 4

INGREDIENTS

1.5 cups zucchini

1.5 cups yellow squash

Spray oil optional

DIRECTIONS

STEP 1

Squash and zucchini should be diced into small bits. Place the zucchini and squash pieces in the air fryer basket. Spray with oil and shake the basket to spread everything evenly.

STEP 2

Cook squash and zucchini in the air fryer at 400 degrees F for about 15 minutes. When cooking, shake the basket to keep it from sticking.

STEP 3

Immediately serve and enjoy!

Artichoke Hearts

Prep Time: 9 mins Cook Time: 7 mins Total time: 16 mins Servings: 4

INGREDIENTS

1 can quartered artichoke hearts, drained

1/8 teaspoon garlic powder

1/4 teaspoon salt

1 tablespoon olive oil

1/8 teaspoon ground black pepper

1/4 teaspoon Italian seasoning

2 teaspoons grated Parmesan cheese

DIRECTIONS

STEP 1

Preheat the air fryer to 400 F.

STEP 2

To remove extra moisture from the artichoke hearts, pat them dry with a paper towel and place them in a basin.

STEP 3

Add Italian seasoning, Parmesan cheese, pepper, salt, and garlic powder. Toss with a little of olive oil.

STEP 4

Cook it for 4 minutes in the air fryer basket. After 4 minutes, shake the basket and cook for another 4 minutes, or until the artichokes begin to brown and the edges are crispy. Serve right away.

CHAPTER SIX

JUICE & SMOOTHIES

Super Skin Glow Juice

INGREDIENTS

1 apple

1 orange, halved and peeled

4 carrots

1/2 cucumber, peeled

A thumb-size piece of ginger

1/2 lemon, peeled

Water, to dilute

Healthy sweetener of choice, to taste

DIRECTIONS

STEP 1

Juice all the ingredients. If the juice has to be thinned, add some water.

STEP 2

Add healthy sweetener of choice (optional).

Pomegranate juice

INGREDIENTS

2 cups pomegranate seeds

1 cup still water

Pinch salt

2 teaspoons sugar optional

DIRECTIONS

STEP 1

In a blender, combine 2 cups pomegranate seeds and process for 10 seconds. Don't keep your pulse going for too long.

STEP 2

Sieve out the juice into a bowl. Use a spoon to press the seeds down so that all the juice can come out.

STEP 3

Put 1 cup of water to the filtered juice and add a pinch of salt and sugar. Mix and Serve chilled.

Strawberry Watermelon Smoothie

INGREDIENTS

1 cup (128g) strawberries hulled and halved

2 cups (256g) frozen watermelon cubes

Maple syrup to taste optional

6 mint leaves optional

DIRECTIONS

STEP 1

In a high-powered blender, combine frozen watermelon strawberries and water. Mint leaves and maple syrup should be added at this point.

STEP 2

Blend until mixture reaches smoothie consistency. Pour into glasses and enjoy.

Coconut Green Smoothie

INGREDIENTS

1 peeled frozen banana chopped

3 tablespoon blanched almonds

75 g (1 cup) spinach

250 ml (1 cup) coconut water

75 g (1/2 cup) frozen blueberries

DIRECTIONS

STEP 1

Place all the ingredients in a blender (high-powered) and blend until smooth. Serve.

Banana Cashew Smoothie

INGREDIENTS

2 ripe bananas peeled

Lemon juice to taste

1/2 cup raw cashews

Handful of ice

240 ml 1 cup almond milk

1 soft pitted date

1 tablespoon chia seeds optional

DIRECTIONS

STEP 1

Blend all of the ingredients in a (high-powered) blender until the cashews are smooth and creamy.

Cucumber Juice

INGREDIENTS

1 whole Cucumber

1-2 Lime or lemon

2 tablespoons honey

3 cups Water

Ice Optional

DIRECTIONS

STEP 1

Juice the lime and put it aside.

STEP 2

Cut the cucumber and add to a food processor or blender, then put water and honey.

STEP 3

Blend or pulse till smooth then sieve through a cheese cloth into a bowl.

STEP 4

Pour the juice into a jar then add the lime juice and stir. Serve on ice immediately or put in the fridge to chill.

Super Green Juice

INGREDIENTS

2 to 3 kale leaves, to taste

2 small cucumbers, peeled

Large handful of spinach

1/2 lemon, peeled, deseeded

1/2 lime, peeled, deseeded

1 1- inch cube of peeled ginger

1 head romaine

2 celery stalks

1 small bunch of parsley, trimmed

DIRECTIONS

STEP 1

In a juicer, combine all of the ingredients listed above.

STEP 2

Serve, refrigerate, or freeze immediately.

Asparagus Juice

INGREDIENTS

6 fat organic spears of asparagus

DIRECTIONS

STEP 1

Wash the asparagus very well.

STEP 2

Remove white ends. Cut into pieces and place it in the juicer.

STEP 3

Pour into glasses. Serve chilled.

Green Pepper Juice

INGREDIENTS

1 green bell peppers

2 carrots

2 lemons (juiced)

1 cucumber

DIRECTIONS

STEP 1

Wash all the vegetables very well.

STEP 2

Peel off the cucumber and carrots.

STEP 3

Cut the stalk of the green bell pepper.

STEP 4

All of the ingredients can be juiced in a juicing machine, or all of the ingredients can be combined in a blender with half a cup of water and blended for 30 seconds. Serve.

Salad In a Glass

INGREDIENTS

1/2 Head romaine lettuce

1 Tomato

2 Celery ribs

1 Carrot, topped

1 Small red bell pepper

DIRECTIONS

STEP 1

Juice all veggies together.

STEP 2

Add salt and pepper to taste (optional)

Printed in Great Britain
by Amazon